Warren Holden

Spiritual Evolution

Warren Holden

Spiritual Evolution

ISBN/EAN: 9783337333256

Printed in Europe, USA, Canada, Australia, Japan

Cover: Foto ©Lupo / pixelio.de

More available books at **www.hansebooks.com**

BY

WARREN HOLDEN,

AUTHOR OF ''FOURTEEN SONNETS,'' ''SONG OF THE SEA,''
AND ''AUTOBIOGRAPHY OF LOVE.''

———————

PHILADELPHIA:

PRESS OF J. B. LIPPINCOTT COMPANY.

1889.

PREFACE.

The too literal interpretation of the Sacred Scriptures exposes them to the assaults of infidelity and atheism.

In order to rescue the Bible from such profane handling, it is necessary to reconcile its apparent self-contradictions; and nothing, it seems to the present writer, can do this so effectually as the unreserved recognition of its symbolic character.

Some examples of symbolism are given in the following verses.

CONTENTS.

9

PRELUDE.

Irreverent wits deride the Holy Word.

It seems at variance with common sense;

And seems to countenance such gross offence,

As makes its claim to holiness absurd.

Of Æsop's fables have they never heard?

How Wisdom aims her lessons to convey

By trite examples, offered every day,

So plain that simple souls need not have erred.

All sacred history is apologue,

Involving meanings for the time concealed,

But, when their aid is opportune, revealed,

From wheels of progress to remove a clog.

Thus trivial fact becomes momentous truth,
And graceless acts of stubborn human will
A mystic part are destined to fulfil:
So graceful form grows out of shape uncouth.

To make free agents serve against their will,
Yet own their vaunted freedom quite intact,
And feel responsible for every act,
Attests God's infinite resource and skill.

To make self-will its prejudice resign,
To make self-love its private aims forego,
And all its goods in charity bestow,
Is the last victory of love divine.

Stript of disguise, 'tis virtually taught
That, man's creation proving a mistake,
A total change the Lord was pleased to make
Of hasty plans,—an obvious after-thought.

Shall the dull clay presume to criticise,
Unknowing what the potter hath designed?
Or shall vain man unfold his Maker's mind,
But dimly pictured to prophetic eyes?

The primal Adam was the embryo man,
Perfected manhood's rude predictive type.
The second Adam, when the time is ripe,
Appears, to consummate creation's plan.

The mere phenomenal most men can know,
Which providences day by day create,
As step by step we march to meet our fate
By gradual paths of evolution slow.

So you're an evolutionist, cries one.
True evolution takes its rise within,
As cobwebs from their bowels spiders spin;
As shadows follow motions of the sun.

God is the active evolutionist.

Men see his shadow and "Eureka" cry;

Life's *modus operandi* think they spy,—

All things evolve themselves, and thus exist.

First let them seek God's kingdom in the soul;

Submit, like little children, to be led;

With wisdom from above be meekly fed;

And inward order will to sight unroll.

CREATOR.

From the beginning the " I Am" is One.
And this " I Am" is love, and love is life.
With love supreme the Universe is rife.
By love alone creation's work is done.

Love's omnipresence doth all things embrace;
Omniscience all things great and small doth scan.
His form is human ; he is primal man,
But yet unlimited by time or space.

By Wisdom Love doth active good invent.
Father and Son inform the Holy Ghost.
Like soul and body in one aim engrossed,
These three are One: the trine omnipotent.

CREATURE.

Love said to Wisdom, let us make mankind.

Our image and our likeness they must share :

Give, therefore, Will and Understanding, where

Wisdom and Love may fitly be enshrined.

As of themselves the godlike race shall seem

To know the good and freely choose the right,

Led by apparent whims of self-delight ;

While heaven's far-sighted aim is to redeem.

CREATION.

Let there be light ! A million suns appear :

The splendid proxies of that central sun,

Which closely veils the unapproachéd One,

Whose heat would all consume if felt too near.

These suns were fit alembics to resolve

Love's fire and crystallize in many an earth,

Adapted for preliminary birth,

While man's creation slowly might evolve.

16

EDEN.

When geologic epochs are complete,
And the bare earth is clothed with verdant spring,
How sweet the morning stars together sing,
While Eden waits her bridal guests to greet :

And all the sons of God shout with delight ;
For restless nomad now may cease to roam,
Since wedded love hath found a garden home,
Where innocence may blossom free from blight.

A cycle of beatitude begun,
The golden age flew by on facile wing,
The kindreds took no thought for anything,
But passed from earth to heaven and deemed them one.

THE FALL.

The tribe, which Adam's name doth symbolize,
Must now be weaned and taught to go alone;
Or else remain a baby overgrown,
The tender nursling of indulgent skies.

E'en as a boy must leave his father's roof,
Like new-made knight with oriflamb unfurled,
To try conclusions with the outside world,
And put his budding manhood to the proof:

So must forecasting Providence exclude
The young race from the cradle of its birth,
To sally forth and grapple with the earth,
A wilderness of passions unsubdued.

LOST INNOCENCE.

Oh, blissful days of early innocence,
Ere sleeping passion dreamed of snares to dread,
Or harpy lusts upon life's banquet fed ;
When unseen guardians hovered in defence,
And angel-whispers came unquestioned whence ;
While stars propitious kindly influence shed ;
Oh, halcyon days, are ye forever fled? ·
And am I quite cast off by Providence?

Crude childhood's innocence is but the root
Whence late developing experience grows.
Betwixt the germ of promise and the fruit
Life's patient years of culture interpose,
Removing noxious weed and straggling shoot,
Till wisdom's innocence maturely glows.

EVOLUTION.

Creation is the building of a man;

A house not made with hands on mortal plan;

A temple where the God of heaven may dwell,

Its architecture could no weird foretell.

To fashion man in God's similitude,

A creature with creative powers endued,

A character of all perfections blent;

Betokens handicraft omnipotent.

For man is not a mere automaton,

By sleight of cunning showman played upon.

Destined as of himself a part to act,

Slowly evolving truth from naked fact,

Life's problems he must one by one forethink,

Forging the chain of being link by link.

THE FLOOD.

The self-sufficient youth would go unchecked :
He takes the bit between his teeth stiff-necked.'

A skilful rider gives his charger rein,
Feeling the freedom of his native plain,
With pride the Arab tosses high his head,
And spurns the ground beneath disdainful tread,
Unmindful of the check that bides its time,
Ready to sober arrogance sublime.

So came the flood upon the rampant youth,
To curb his bold defiance of the truth.
On Shinar's plain ambition prostrate lies,
Where Babel's tower aspired to scale the skies.

THE PRODIGAL.

Self-confidence must run its reckless race,

Self-providence must end in bankruptcy,

Or prodigal will ne'er his steps retrace,

And humbly seek paternal wisdom's knee.

The groping race must find its only friend

Through many ups and downs of seeming ill

And seeming good, subserving one main end,

Their Maker's service with spontaneous will.

IDOLATRY.

To idol-worship man is ever prone.

To rectify the vicious native bent,

By adequate reward and punishment,

From Abram down; the will of God is shown.

But the great mass was superstition's tool.

Yet these were nearer truth than the wise fool

Whose shallow heart hath said " there is no God."

No God! Why not no sun, no sea, no land

Besieging every sense on every hand?

Nature with all her voices utters "God."

Dependence is the burden of her vow.

This of necessity implies a God,

A power above to which all knees must bow,

Uplifting man above the senseless clod;

A Providence that orders our defence,

Whose sovereign sway commands our reverence.

No revelation needs to make us know

A *God;* but only the *true* God to show.

The counterfeit implies the genuine.

A suckling may mistake its proper dam,

And may be well contented with the sham;

But never doubts the proper dam hath been.

The beastly bushman and the sceptic grand

Are fellow-atheists of kindred mind,

Deaf to faith's still small voice from spirit land,

To hope's irradiant rainbow color-blind.

These rare exceptions but confirm the rule,

Intuitive belief, whatever school.

From Egypt there goes up a cry of pain,
God's chosen people groaning under reign
Of sin and self, taskmasters full of pride.
In his own household man's worst foes reside.

The force of circumstance who weakly pleads
Shall be a servant's servant evermore.
Who says the woman in temptation leads
Is fit for stripes. To laughter give him o'er.

Each soul must stand or fall by his own deed.
Yet God is merciful as man hath need.
A bruised reed he shall not rudely break
And smoking flax he shall not coldly quench;
But keep the feeblest spark of truth awake,
The weakest will of virtue strong intrench.

So God took council on his people's side,
And chose a man of God to be their guide.

CORRESPONDENCE.

To gain the sanctuary of the Word,

Refer each outward act to inward cause.

Learn to interpret spiritual laws :

Voices within the veil may then be heard.

Let Egypt signify the natural heart,

With Moses and the host on either part ;

And meanings full of pith may be inferred.

Thus Pharaoh, representing natural sense,

And roughly ruling the mind's kingdom thence,

Plague-smitten hardly lets the people go

To worship God the way his precepts show.

Then Moses leads them, fighting all along
With desert armies of temptation strong.
Pillar of fire by night and cloud by day,
A mystic banner, guides their doubtful way.

At every stage some enemies they slew.
The Red Sea swallowed up a wicked crew.
Gaunt famine fed her fill, and pestilence
Stalked in the darkness, mocking at defence;
While dire destruction wasted in broad day,
Scorpions and fiery serpents spread dismay.

O human heart, thou cage of unclean birds,
Thou den of evil beasts, few be thy words.

But Moses pleased not God at Horeb's rock,

Reluctant with his rod the springs to unlock.

The promised land forbid, from Pisgah's height

He views: a symbol, in its fruitful soil,

Of blessedness reserved for man's delight,

When the new heavens and earth divide their spoil.

The ceremonial law was but a school

To discipline the heart for Christ's mild rule.

Spontaneous love his new commandment brings.

At his behest faith's living waters flow,

A well that from the heart forever springs;

And dead formalities unmissed may go.

There was a boy on far Judea's hills
Who kept his father's sheep. His story fills
Full many a page of sacred history.
The first page solves his fortune's mystery.

Joy waits upon his steps from morn till eve;
And peace prepares the dreams his slumbers weave.

The sun arose to represent the throne
Of Deity in dazzling splendor shown.
He worshipped there with soul and body prone.

In milder beauty sank the evening sun,
Bedecked with robe of many colors spun.
Again he bowed and made his orison.

While on the blazoned shield that shelters night,
Whose stars betoken truth and honor bright,
He read his destiny in signs of light.

He knew no fear, because he knew no sin,

Content to let the Master rule within.

To meet a bear and lion in the way,

And with his hands alone the beasts to slay,

For such a boy was merely rugged play.

To hurl a boastful giant headlong down,

And burst the bubble of his false renown,

Enough a shepherd's sling and polished stone,

By hand of innocence and trust if thrown.

No false pretence his honor could betray,

For he had learned to love and to obey.

Obedience was his proper name; and love,—

Love and obedience, names revered above.

Thou happy shepherd boy! Oh, hapless day,
When needful service called the boy away
And made of him a conqueror and king:
As if that office were the one grand thing.

Thrice happier the simple shepherd boy
Than all the kings in one; with all their joy
Of gold and gauds and ceremonial rites,
And lawless power and sensuous delights,
That ever gratified the shallow heart
Of grown-up children. Must we ever part,
My David? Oh, come back, boy of the soul,
And be the model of young self-control.

31

And David fought the battles of the Lord,

Who gave the kings as dust unto his sword.

Saul slew his thousands: David ten times more,

Triumphing gloriously o'er and o'er.

And David's harp could soothe the wrath of Saul;

From evil spirit gently disenthrall.

His skilful fingers could the raptures raise

Of humble hope and joy and pious praise,

And ring the changes of the heart's wild ways.

"Man after God's own heart" though grand his style,

Yet for a moment heeding subtle wile

Of the sly serpent, self; he fell,—how low!

A common sinner could no lower go.

Ah, who has any strength in his own right?

The moment man lets go his hold on God,

He sinks into the black abyss of night.

Thence painful paths of penitence are trod,

Ere he may dare look up in heaven's pure sight.

Out of the depths do I cry unto thee :

Hear me, O Lord ; attend the voice of my prayer.

If thou, O Lord, shouldst mark iniquity,

Lord, who shall stand ? But 'tis thy right to spare.

My waiting soul forgiveness hopes to share.

SOLOMON.

In dreams the heart betrays its real aim.

Dreams hold a mirror to the naked breast,

Revealing all we secretly love best,

Whether it be our glory or our shame.

Happy the man who shrinks not from the view.

King Solomon thus made his famous choice.

The land of Israel might 'well rejoice

When that propitious dream was proven true.

So God made Solomon the wisest man,

To judge with equity and rule with ease;

Both good and evil, friend and foe to please;

And added wealth that human wish outran.

Solomon's fame was like a meteor hurled

Blazing abroad, the wonder of the world.

Yet a mere child, that knows but to obey,

Shall better keep the straight and narrow way.

PARABLE.

If scripture, when interpreted aright,
Includes all your profound philosophy,
Why not lay bare the truth to common sight?

Deep truth, when sown in simple, childlike minds,
To whom appearance is reality,
Assimilates the scanty soil it finds.

We suffer children to believe their eyes,
Nor torture them with knowledge premature,—
Old heads upon young shoulders in disguise.

Races, like them, must creep before they walk,
And gradually make their footing sure.
So too they lisp before they plainly talk.

The simple facts as final truths to see
In scriptures given to a forming race,
Is like defending, with a serious face,
Each nursery tale as valid history.

Nature and human history are true
As vehicles of deep interior things,
Only because the shifting shadow brings
Semblance of hidden substance into view.

No mere fantastic myth is symbolism.
It grows as orderly as flower from seed.
Systematized, it forms a perfect creed,
All consecrated by a holy chrism.

NATURE.

Thou solemn wood, fair hill, and pleasant stream
Befringed with flowers, why do we love you so?
Our yearning hearts along your pathways go
As if enchanted in a blissful dream.
And things inanimate all living seem;
While bounteous Nature's lap doth overflow
With goodly gifts her lavish hands bestow
To crown our lives with happiness supreme.

Nature is rooted in the human soul.
She springeth from the seed that man hath sown;
And owes her growth to his occult control.
Our fickle moods induce her changing tone:
A part of us, her life reflects our own,
Each part a typic semblance of the whole.

MACROCOSM AND MICROCOSM.

There's beauty everywhere. The azure sky,

The golden sun that fills the world with light,

The moon and stars that glorify the night;

The smiling earth with mountains towering high,

And lowly vales between that sleeping lie;

Lake, river, fall, and ocean flashing bright,

Prairie and forest wild with flowers bedight;

And all reflected in the human eye, —

The many-colored mirror of the soul,

Which sees itself in every new disguise,

In every picture, every quaint design

The world's wide panorama may unroll.

The meditative eye shall recognize

Each shade of beauty as a trait divine.

WATER.

Around the lake spellbound we idly stray,
Or trace the streamlet, dwindling to a rill,
Through mead and vale up to its parent hill,
Whence forth it starts upon its winding way.
The river widely roaming finds the bay,
Where rest the wearied argosies so still,
Escaped from conflict with the ocean's will,
That claims intruders for his lawful prey.

Around the world the sparkling waters roll,
Conveying health and wealth to every part;
The circulating system of the earth:
So truth divine, the life-blood of the soul,
Shall spring perennial in the human heart,
A living well, baptismal of new birth.

MOUNTAINS.

O height sublime, whose fascinating spell

Can lure the pilgrim up thy rugged side,

Upon thy top near heaven let me abide,

Above the line where clouds of passion dwell.

Thy crystal atmosphere shall gently quell

The rage of feverish care and frantic pride;

While faith beholds a vision glorified,

And raptures, awe-inspired, the bosom swell.

Mount Sinai, thou type of holy fear,

Thunder and lightning bode thy threatening rod.

Pisgah surveys the land of promised cheer.

A chosen few the mount of glory trod.

Mount Olivet to Jesus' memory dear.

Fair Zion's hill, the dwelling-place of God.

God has all power or else he were no god.
But with discretion must he use his might,
In strict observance of the creature's right;
Not use it like a Jove's capricious nod.

To fashion man by archetype so high,—
An image and a likeness of himself,—
He needs must humor the conceited elf,
His freedom's jealous pride must pacify.

You prate of human liberty, and tell
How gracious God designed that man be free;
And brand as his most bitter enemy
The villain who that liberty would sell.

Yet spite of all your promise in the bud,
And spite of all your boasted Providence,
The history of liberty's defence
Is written in her martyred votaries' blood.

Rulers have claimed divine authority
To limit subjects to a beaten path,
To dictate faith, interpret heaven's decree,
And punish calcitrants with human wrath. ˙

Dissenters have been objects of contempt,
Imprisoned, mulcted, scourged for conscience' sake ;
Heretics tortured and burned at the stake,
All in God's name, by pharisees who dreamt
That they were favorites, and bent the knee
In thanks for heaven's supposed venality.

If God loves liberty, why doth he not
Bury beneath an avalanche of shame
The tricksters who belie his holy name
To justify their hypocritic plot?

Hold, zealous righter of all human wrong.

I pray you bridle up your too hot haste,

And let not useful energies run waste.

God doth not so because true God is strong.

Perceive you not how patience infinite

Shields the integrity of human wit,

Which thou wouldst instantly destroy because

Forsooth 'tis not controlled by thy wise laws?

But freedom's .God permits such hypocrites

To think they wield his thunder-bolt of wrath.

Thou simpleton, no vengeance mercy hath.

Love is God's only weapon, as befits.

All wrath is man's device, and sin betrays.

But God shall make the wrath of man his praise.

Thou Son of God, who died that we might live,

Teach us thy hardest lesson,—to forgive.

Freedom is ours: and ours its foul abuse.
Ages' experience must teach its use.

Although reflection force us to infer
That man is merely as the potter's clay
· Moulded by the divine Artificer:

Yet must. man feel quite uncontrolled by fate
To shape his course in his own wilful way,
Or forfeit manhood's most distinctive trait.

Why tell a man he's free, with freedom's tide
Bounding through every vein? With freedom's breath
Fresh every moment from hope's mountain-side?
What questions he of thraldom's living death?

PARADOX.

He knows he's free: but then he knows as well,
Unless God ruled, the Universe were hell.

The spiritual paradox; resolved
Somehow by superhuman calculus:
The differentiated infinite,
Into innumerable atoms split,
Becomes fragmental man with time involved.
The integrated finite, God-with-us.

In fact, the finite and the infinite
Are opposites, exclusive each to each.
Yet constant intercourse must bridge the breach,
However unexplained by human wit. ~

Truce then to childish fantasy that God
Could if he would save man in his own spite.
Coöperation is creation's might ;
Man fills his rôle or life's a stage untrod.

Yet boasted freedom's but a borrowed boat,

Re-borrowed daily bankrupts chance to float.

Let him beware of that accruing debt

With usance, if fair gain he fail to get.

That debtor's prison hath no 'scaping door,

Till the last farthing of the debt's paid o'er;

False steps retraced where feet unheeding rove,

The web of wilful wickedness unwove.

Doth not our rich and generous creditor

Freely forgive the debt? What thence infer?

Can debt forgiven reclothe a naked soul,

Whose garment in time's loom is woven whole?

And woven only by his own right hand,

As day by day supplies each single strand?

Unto himself the debt is mainly due.

Then to himself let every soul be true,

Seeking true riches, careless of mere pelf;

And heaven will help the soul that helps himself.

ADVENT. "THE HOUR BEFORE DAWN."

Watchman, what of the night? The clouds increase,

And all around grows darker and more drear.

Our hearts within are failing us for fear,

And hope deferred is pining for release.

Why lingers the long-promised Prince of Peace,

Messiah sent to bring salvation near,

To free the captive, broken hearts to cheer,

Of sin and sorrow to command surcease?

The Bridegroom lingers and our hearts grow faint,

Waiting with longing eyes the dawning light;

Our lamps go out, our limbs the cold benumbs.

Is there no ear to hear man's piteous plaint?

Watchman, what of the night? What of the night?

The watchman saith: Behold, the Bridegroom comes.

Hail, highly favored one; of women blest:

Thy virgin bosom heaven doth consecrate

To nurse the infant Christ to man's estate.

Thus Gabriel announced the high behest;

And sweet surprise thy modest heart confessed.

The weary nations need no longer wait

To find the master-key of human fate,

The long expectant ages' promised rest.

Enough to ponder in thy quiet heart:

All generations blesséd calling thee,

The lowly handmaid raised to honor's part.

From Eve's hereditary sorrow free,

The happiest of womankind thou art,

The mother of the Son of God to be.

CHRISTMAS.

The doom impending o'er a fallen race
By love miraculous is charmed away;
For unto us a child is born this day,
Whose innocence shall mortal guilt replace.
All hail! Thou wonder of redeeming grace!
The sheep forlorn in wilderness astray
Their rightful shepherd's voice will now obey,
And all their weary wanderings retrace.

Thou babe divine, no language can express
The boundless mother-love that worships thee,
Bringing its gifts, the tribute of the heart.
To hold thee clasped in reverent caress,
And serve thy simple needs on bended knee,
Or watch thy sleep: could heaven more bliss impart?

THE MASSACRE OF THE INNOCENTS.

In Rama was there heard the voice of tears,

Of Rachel weeping for her children slain,

Refusing comfort, since no more she hears

Prattle that tells the tale of summers twain.

Egypt gave refuge to the Holy One;

For out of Egypt God hath called his Son.

Regeneration leads from Egypt's night

Through wilderness of sin to Canaan's light.

So when King Herod paid the debt of death,

The angel of the Lord brought Joseph word.

Recall from exile joyfully they heard,

And came with haste and dwelt in Nazareth.

I dreamed it was my happy destiny

To guide the tender Christ in worldly ways;

Explain the sights that filled him with amaze,

And smooth his first rough steps towards Calvary.

The aureole revealed divinity,

Crowning his brow with mildly beaming rays.

His docile mien and far-off wistful gaze

Had moved severest mentor's clemency.

Awake, I was a teacher of rude boys.

Thenceforth I saw them with indulgent eyes,

Partaking heartily their simple joys:

Nor sought to make them prematurely wise,

But drew them out with innocent decoys;

For each one seemed the Christ-child in disguise.

Know ye that wondrous boy of Holy Writ,

How 'mid the doctors he did meekly sit,

Hearing their grave discourse with eager ears,

And asking questions far beyond his years?

About his father's business much concerned

Ere other boys the alphabet have learned

Of useful service. Happy Nazareth boys,

His playmates, sharing more than common joys.

Wistful and curious ye would search his face,

When some profounder feeling left its trace.

Honoring as father one of David's line,

Yet hearing whispers of a sire divine,—

Whispers prophetic of his dire crusade

Against the powers of darkness,—undismayed

He reached the stature of his heritage,

Ripe to begin his painful pilgrimage.

The Holy Spirit must unloose the tongue

That would dilate the story, which hath rung

Through heaven's high courts the countless choirs among,

A song of wonder more than half unsung.

52.

"VOICE FROM THE WILDERNESS."

Now dawn dispels the night-of-time's despair.

The wilderness reveals a youth discreet,

Whose heart is love, his tongue truth's bitter-sweet.

His outer garment is of camel's hair ;

The robe of righteousness his soul doth wear.

Though locusts and wild honey are his meat,

Each word proceeding from the mercy-seat,

The bread of life, his choice of daily fare.

He preached repentance,—change in point of view.

For *man* self-centred, *God* as central sun,

Adjusting man's abnormal attitude.

When each his destined orbit traces true,

The reign of chaos ends, Christ's will is done,

His kingdom come, and all the earth renewed.

NEW TRUTH.

The keen-eyed watchman on fair Zion's wall
On far horizon spies a stranger knight,
Whose banner, glancing in the morning light,
Displays a new device, unknown to all.

Challenged, his tongue trips up on "Shibboleth."
At once the watchman cries out "heretic!"
The imitative people answer quick,
Reëchoing the charge with bated breath.

Few care to sift and prove the heresy.
One has his farm, and one his merchandise.
Do they not pay experts to use their eyes,
And keep their patrons from such trouble free?

So with no chance to break a lance in fight,
But harried in detraction's wicked way,
And to its secret dagger left a prey,
Lies foully done to death the stranger knight.

TEMPTATIONS.

When Christ had fasted forty painful days,
The tempter came and made his bold assays.

Thou Son of God, transform these stones to bread.
The bread you wot cannot my hunger feed,
My yearning love to succor human need.
Save by God's word that hunger is unfed.

Behold the glory of this world of mine!
Here worship me and all this power is thine.
False fiend, the kingdoms are not thine to give;
And man must worship God if he would live.

Cast thyself down; 'tis written, angel bands
Have charge of thee, and in their gentle hands
Shall bear thee up, lest thou encounter harm.
In vain the devil tries each subtle charm
To tempt the Lord his God with purpose base;
Baffled he leaves, and angels take his place.

CHANGING WATER TO WINE.

At Cana's marriage, when they wanted wine,

Christ simply ordered water from the well.

And though he used no necromantic spell,

The water changed to choicest fruit o' the vine.

Water and wine, two forms of truth the same,

Are interchangeable in wisdom's name.

One substance underlies the divers forms

Of Nature, whose vitality it warms.

Thus Jesus' mighty miracles began.

Glory to God he gave; good-will to man.

PURIFICATION OF THE TEMPLE.

Make not my Father's house a house of gain,

He said; and scourged them from their trade profane.

My house is rightly called the house of prayer.

The people bring their humble offerings there;

And grace and peace the contrite heart receives.

But ye have made my house a den of thieves.

Since thou assum'st prerogative divine,

Prove thine authority by certain sign.

Destroy this temple, and within three days,

Again its fair proportions I will raise.

This temple hath been building many a year;

Which thou forsooth in three days wouldst uprear.

But Jesus spake of the soul's sacred shrine,

The human body, meant henceforth to shine

With God's indwelling. Mystic words he said,

Explained when he was risen from the dead.

Rabbi, thou art a teacher come from God;
Thy miracles attest Messiah's rod.

Who sees God's kingdom must be born again.
How can a man be born when he is old?
That which is born of flesh is fleshly men,
But spirit claims a spiritual mould.

Life's not the inheritance of earth-born flesh.
The dead can neither purchase life nor sell.
The natural life is but the outer shell
To keep the growing kernel sweet and fresh.

Why marvel at the thought of second birth,
When miracles abound throughout the earth?

The unfamiliar seems miraculous;
Familiar things are parts of nature's course.
Let Reason trace them to their primal source,
And she may find their true relations thus.

The wind blows where it will, ye know not whence.

A valid miracle in consequence.

Maturer sense shall tell both whence and how;

Then none will stare at weather-change as now.

They'll station men upon the mountain-tops .

To signal how to manage ships and crops.

Allowing then that wind is only air

In motion set by heat-waves here and there,

Whence do the waves of heat derive their force?

Thus backward step by step the wonder moves,

Driven to its last retreat, its hidden source,

Till God at length the only wonder proves.

Should miracle be razed from wisdom's page

As superstition of a darker age?

Nay, since from God at last all things derive,

It follows miracles perennial thrive.

Life is a miracle in every phase.

The seed springs up and grows in secret ways.

Observing laws ye cannot understand,

Ye plant and think it grows at your command.

CAUSE AND EFFECT.

In what precedes a thing its cause ye see.

As if by cause and its effect were meant

Mere antecedent and its consequent.

Heaven laughs at such unripe philosophy.

Both are effects of unknown spirit laws.

External things have in themselves no cause.

All nature is the realm of dead effects,

The shadow that interior truth projects.

Constant precedence, that so looks like cause,

And to the natural reason so appeals,

Argues that truths conform to serial laws,

Their shadows following hard upon their heels:

As panoramic pictures on a screen

In sequence like the originals are seen.

SCIENCE AND FAITH.

Science demands your proofs with accent rough.

The unsophisticated heart believes.

·Its own spontaneous faith is proof enough.

And what do all your boasted proofs avail;

Hypotheses, whose sandy base deceives,

And any change of weather may assail?

Conditions change: grave science changes base,

And calmly reconstructs; new cobwebs weaves,

Without misgiving or a change of face.

But the heart's hope is founded on a rock,

That hath withstood the interminable shock

Of infidelity in every form,

And still secure abides the angry storm.

-

Facts are the outward clothing of the mind.

They may be donned and doffed as climates change,

With new condition, fashions, manners strange.

But still the unchanging truth remains behind.

Facts are forgotten or are quite disproved.

The truths they witness suffer no decay,

But find new habitations every day,

Their deep foundations evermore unmoved.

Parable, fable, fiction, solid fact,

Which justly show how sacred truth may act,

Are welcome equally in wisdom's sight.

Let choice of vehicle be left to chance

From stage to stage, if thus the soul advance

Upon her journey towards the realms of light.

To find out God unaided Reason fails:

Therefore, of course, there is no God, she rails.

Eyes cannot hear, therefore there is no sound;

Ears have no sight, therefore no light is found.

To Reason's search the book of truth is sealed.

She can but recognize a truth revealed;

Adumbrate truth by bringing fact to view.

From faith alone can Reason take her cue.

She hath no warrant to originate.

Belief in God is the heart's postulate:

Inwoven in the texture of the soul,

Love's warp entwines faith's woof in seamless whole.

FAITH AND CREED.

Misuse of terms, careless or ignorant,

Full many a root of bitterness may plant.

Apples of discord are the natural fruit

To be developed from such hybrid shoot.

In popular locution faith and creed

Are synonymes: confusion fit to breed

Successive armies of Quixotic knights,

Armed *cap-a-pie* for controversial fights.

Creed is a creature of the intellect,

And finds embodiment in varied sect.

Faith is the offspring of the obedient heart,

The work of charity its chosen part.

Creed is repellent, cordial faith invites;

The one divides, the other close unites.

Creed is observant of cold rigid form.

Faith kindles the spontaneous prayers that warm.

Men write out creeds and publish them in books.

Faith speaks its messages in living looks.

To set up creeds is human wisdom's boast.

Faith is the free gift of the Holy Ghost.

To break the ten commandments outwardly,
As simple denizens of space and time:
To lie, defraud, to steal or kill, is crime
Against the organized community.

.

To break the ten commandments from within,
To steal away another's truth and good,
In heart deny the rights of brotherhood,
Or claim Christ's merit as our own; is sin.

.

Men punish crime for safety of the whole.
But sin is secret, only known to God.
Confess to him and humbly kiss the rod;
But let no stranger meddle with thy soul.

,

.

LAW.

Man is the subject of unchanging law.

' Obey a law and reap a sure reward.

Transgress a law, it straight becomes a sword.

Wherein you fail, find in yourself the flaw.

Omnipotence itself cannot withdraw

The sentence unbribed justice bids record.

Law's of the very essence of the Lord.

Man can but bow submissive and in awe.

To thrive by favor is the fool's fond hope.

To foster favorites is the vice of kings,

And marks the meanness despotism brings.

Then pray for guidance only, and for light;

And pray for help with anarchy to cope.

God's law is ever on the side of right.

PRAYER.

Since God's unchangeable, why storm his throne
With unavailing eloquence of prayer?
The devotee his worship may forbear;
As well do homage to a stock or stone.
Let men of mind discard the suppliant's tone,
Assume the stoic's unimpassioned air;
If need be, make a virtue of despair,
And undergo the load of life alone.

The clouds, that hide the sun's incessant cheer,
Spring from the earth. Soon as the wind's deft hand
Withdraws the curtain, smiles will reappear.
The sun of love never averts his face.
Mists of self-love shut out the heavenly grace.
Prayer lifts the veil; and lo the vision grand.

"IN HIM WE LIVE AND MOVE AND HAVE OUR BEING."

God is the all in all of souls that be.

His only life inspires love's passionate breath;

His truth reveals each word that wisdom saith;

He is the inner light by which we see.

Man's wiles unwitting work out God's decree;

Into each secret thought he entereth.

Where God inhabits not, is merely death.

Yet self-willed man still boasts his action free.

Man's seeming independence serves the end

Of forwarding heaven's ultimate design,

Towards which apparent opposites all tend,—

To lift humanity from low to high,

God's image and his likeness multiply,

And blend in one the human and divine.

PANTHEISM.

Wherefore doth kindly Providence allow
The prodigal to wander off so far,
With monstrous sins his innocence to mar,
And wallow with the swine in selfhood's slough?
Why not compel the youth's reluctant vow,
His wayward wickedness by force debar;
Or fascinate his eye with virtue's star,
Until to God's authority he bow?

Wouldst rest content with Pantheism's reign,
With everlasting sameness to be cloyed?
A firm free footing every soul must gain,
A certain self-support no power can shake,
A something of his own no power can take,
Enough to fill Nirvana's empty void.

Father in heaven, who mak'st thy sun to rise

Alike upon the evil and the good,

How plain the lesson to be understood,

That all are equal in thy holy eyes.

The impartial rain moreover testifies

That just and unjust share thy fatherhood.

If wise or simple, each may know who would

Man's destiny is woven in the skies.

If one sheep of a hundred goes astray,

Doth the good shepherd carelessly resign

The straggling waif to prowling wolves a prey?

Doth he not rather leave the ninety-nine,

And seek the lost one, wander where he may?

Thus saith the Lord: "Behold, all souls are mine."

LIFE AND DEATH.

I am the resurrection and the life.

He that believes in me, though he were dead,

Yet shall he live: and whosoever lives

And still believes in me, shall never die.

Men fret and fume and fancy that they live.

'Tis vain illusion all, a dance of death.

Unless God wills man never draws a breath.

Life is the Deity's prerogative.

Because they seem to work their own self-will,

Men think they order life by private skill.

Permitted farce, a temporary shift.

Our seeming life's a momentary gift.

So when the Lord of life drew nigh the grave,

Death fled before him, coming but to save.

Though four days dead, came Lazarus forth alive.

Christ touched the bier, the widow's son awoke.

He took the damsel's hand, her slumber broke.

Where comes THE LIFE all nature must revive.

The sick, the lame, the blind, the dumb, the maimed,

Lepers and lunatics are all reclaimed.

But greater works than these shall ye achieve.

Naught is impossible if ye believe.

And I will send the holy Comforter;

Perception of the truth shall he confer.

Freely ye shall receive; as freely give.

Speak boldly in my name, the dead shall live.

Through faith ye shall accomplish what ye please.

The very look of love shall heal disease.

With strength divine your hearts to reinforce,

The gates of hell shall not arrest your course.

It is not ye that speak, or act, or will:

My spirit doth the docile bosom fill. ·

Ye only live because my life I lend.

Lo, I am with you alway to the end.

THE PARALYTIC.

My son, thy sins be all forgiven thee.

Who mocketh God? Who speaketh blasphemy?

What difference makes it whether I should say,

Thy sins forgiven, or, Rise and go thy way?

Sickness and sin are but effect and cause,

Related closely by unvarying laws.

My purpose is that my disciples know

The true relationship of high and low.

The Son of man presides with like control

O'er mortal body and immortal soul.

REPENTANCE.

Thy brother brings repentance of the lip.

Though coming oft thou shalt accept his plea.

Thou mayst not judge the heart thou canst not see,

And must not turn from proffered fellowship.

Dost argue thence that God may be cajoled?

Repentance in his sight, who sees the heart,

Is turning from your sins, entire new start:

Evasion cannot pass, however bold.

THE BREAD OF LIFE.

I am the bread of life. Who eats this bread,

Which is my flesh, abides not with the dead.

How can this man give us his flesh to eat?

My flesh and blood are real drink and meat.

Unless ye eat my flesh and drink my blood,

Ye've no indwelling life to outlive death's flood.

Because my flesh is uncreated love,

The living bread that cometh from above,

The food that immortality can nurse,

The sole self-substance of the Universe.

Because my blood is all-pervading truth

That circulates wherever spirit can,

Conveying love, that feeds immortal youth,

To every part of consubstantial man,

Whose perfect whole congenial parts disclose,

The macrocosm that microcosms compose.

CORRESPONDENCE.

The spiritual things of God are seen
Through natural things, revealing what they mean.

The words I speak are spirit in disguise.
The literal sense is but their garb of flesh,
Through which they may appear to earthly eyes.
A flood of light is ready to refresh
Faith-opened eyes; and in my every word
A world of meaning by true ear is heard.

To eat and drink mean to appropriate,
To inwardly digest and make your own.
Man cannot live by earthly bread alone.
Heaven's bread, God's word, sustains the eternal state.

Oft as ye eat and drink, remember me,
And with your daily bread my body break.
My blood, the wine of truth, with thanks partake.
And so shall grow my likeness silently.

How can unwashen hands defile a man?

What entereth the mouth cannot defile.

What cometh from the heart, each thought that's vile,

Sly hint of hypocrite and courtesan;

Envies and jealousies, an evil eye,

Foul blasphemies, whatever makes a lie;

These be the pitch whose touch defiles the heart,

And leaves its smutch upon the inward part.

The inside of the vessel make ye clean.

The outside then will also pure be seen.

Hand-washing follows choice: let conscience bind

In what concerns the washing of the mind.

HUMILITY.

Towards God humility becometh man.
Abject servility belongs to slaves.
Be humble and yet noble if you can;
But sycophancy totally depraves.

Would you have freemen sneaking into grace?
Think you that God delights in aught that's base?
You make God in your own similitude,
And give him attributes as seems you good.

If you are favored, what becomes my plight,
Who ask no favor, claiming only right?
Imagine not that God loves cowardice,
Or any other soul-degrading vice.

No doubt he pities, and in tenderness
Sends chastisement, as love disguised, to bless.
Worship to God, honor to man be shown;
Yet self-respect must firmly hold its own.

CONSISTENCY.

To be consistent one should never change.

The thing that hath been shall forever be.

Let faith and hope and love wait passively

With "Mariana in the moated grange."

Repentance even is beyond the range

Of thorough-going strict consistency.

Rely on old tradition's guarantee.

Leave to adventurers the new and strange.

Thus nightmare warns. What doth the Spirit say?

Think not beforehand what to speak or do.

The heart's spontaneous impulses obey.

The present duty faithfully pursue.

Ignoring past and future, act to-day;

And seeming opposites shall both prove true.

CONFORMITY.

How may the wrangling sects at last agree,

And live thenceforth in mutual harmony?

Meekly submit to one o'ermastering mind.

Choose him as umpire; let his sentence bind.

If some stout protestant still lifts his head,

Stretch him at once on the procrustean bed.

Gain uniformity at any price;

For non-conformity's a vulgar vice.

Infinity evolves variety.

Hence no two human minds are quite alike.

The coiner's die, made by a man, will strike

A thousand coins, each a fac-simile.

Is the Creator like a mere machine?

The artist's patient hand-work will supply

A more germane comparison whereby

God's pains with individuals may be seen.

In charity all parties may agree.

In doctrine every conscience must be free.

INNOCENCE.

Unconscious childhood trips along in glee,

Each attitude displaying native grace.

Beaming with fresh intelligence, the face

In simple confidence looks up to thee.

Accounting innocence life's richest fee,

Why may not manhood run its headlong race,

At careless childhood's easy loitering pace,

And reach the goal from misadventure free?

Each new-fledged soul reveals a thought of God :

A truth in embryo forms its inward parts.

But clogged with selfhood's cloak of sinful flesh,

The world's defiling ways 'tis doomed to plod.

Lord, wash our feet, and bid us start afresh,

Our guide, thy law engraven on our hearts.

LOVE THY NEIGHBOR AS THYSELF.

Attend to thine own business, counsels self:
And straining every nerve, with hungry greed,
To gather ample store of worldly pelf,
Stifles compassion for his brother's need.

Who would be disenthralled must pay the price.
Let other men bestir themselves like me.
I give them good example and advice.
Am I my brother's legalized trustee?

E'en so, thou art thy brother's keeper, Cain.
Thou mayst not hoard thy goods on private shelf.
Count naught thine own that's not his equal gain.
Thou shalt e'en love thy neighbor as thyself.

●

Be good to thine own soul, the miser said:

And double-locked the door-way of his heart.

Accepting favors, he will none impart.

Unblessed with love, in hell he makes his bed.

The lover wooed a maiden; won and led

The blushing bride to Hymen's happy mart.

To prove each other perfect bounds their art.

A narrow round of human bliss they tread.

Who loves another in him doubly lives.

As many loves so many lives has he.

He dwells where'er congenial hearts are found.

The giver, God, himself entirely gives.

He chiefly lives in those his love sets free;

Whence heaven is happiness that knows no bound.

The champions of opposing doctrines fight.

Each claiming victory, they oft renew

The endless battle. What can laymen do

When doctors disagree, and both seem right?

The proverb says that one man's wholesome meat

Another's poison proves. May we not find,

The proper truth to nourish every mind

Requires selection equally discreet?

The man who does God's will, the Saviour said,

Shall know the doctrine, whether it be true.

Simple obedience holds the secret clew

By which the soul life's labyrinth may tread.

Only the pure in heart God's truth perceive;

And with the heart alone the pure believe.

SACRED AND PROFANE.

Some keep religion and philosophy
Partitioned bookcase-like with sliding door.
On opening one, the other's closed the more.
A wise precaution lest they disagree.'

A place for everything, and each in place.
Mixed dialectics is a wild-goose-chase.

Would you be firm in faith, without one doubt?
Then shut your ears; keep controversy out.
Attend one church; repeat its prayers and creed.
Let one sectarian sheet supply your need.

Quoth self-complacency, with lofty ease,
"My mind's made up, say anything you please."
At one ear in, the other out, it goes.
Naught can disturb pure egotism's repose.

A TIME FOR ALL THINGS.

Sunday for God, week-days for man's concerns.

A time for all things; let them take their turns.

Sacred and secular should never mix,

Proprieties time-honored to unfix.

Conduct your business in a business way,

Reserving charity for holiday;

To think of others' claims distracts the mind.

The devil's logic favors his own kind.

DECEITFULNESS OF RICHES.

But where's the profit, though you gain the world,

And lose your soul, in gloomy sheol hurled.

Oh, miserable illusion of great wealth,

Acquired through loss of love, and loss of ease,

And hardening of heart, and legal stealth,

And lust of gain that millions can't appease!

8   85

And for what end? To be the cynosure
Of vulgar gaze, whose praise is insecure.

And though wealth take not wings and fly away,
As oft it wont; it still behind must stay
When we go hence to sojourn here no more,
Far faring to that unreturning shore.

Lay up your everlasting treasures there,
Beyond the reach of rust and cankering care;
True riches, generous love that takes no fee:
For where your treasure is your heart will be.

GOOD STEWARDSHIP.

But thanks to God who rules the human heart,
Not all, like ·Cain, a brother's claims deny.
Some, like Girard, have heard the orphan's cry.
May many choose the blessed giver's part.

The earth, O Lord, is full of riches thine.
Good stewardship is manhood's noblest sign.

PERSONAL SALVATION.

May I but 'scape the yawning jaws of hell,
And safely land within the golden gate,
Secure from further risk of dubious fate,
My rescued soul shall sing: all now is well.
What endless joy the story o'er to tell,
How I was snatched just ere it was too late!
What ecstasies my precious soul await!
To heaven's high throne let hallelujahs swell.

Who then shall fight the battles of the Lord?
Who share the burden of a brother's doom?
Who stem the headlong tide of human ill?
Gird me, I pray, with Gideon's daring sword;
Or bid me make my bed 'mid Hades' gloom,
So I but help to work God's holy will.

TOLERANCE.

We saw, outcasting devils in thy name,

One not of us, whom therefore we forbade.

Forbid him not.   True faith he must have had.

Of Jew or Gentile a good deed's the same.

I'm not the founder of a narrow sect.

In every nation he that doeth good

Asserts his right to Christian brotherhood.

Sincerity's the test of God's elect.

REVENGE.

If Christ were God, why crushed he not his foes?

In conscious triumph asks the infidel.

Because he's God, and not impatient man.

He came the wrath of cruel man to quell;

Not to increase the sum of human woes.

By following out your diabolic plan

The catalogue of human ills would swell,

And sink the soul in deeper depths of hell.

Pray for your enemies.   May they not be

Stray children of your father's family?

WHO IS CHIEF?

Upon his throne the despot swells with pride,

As round him crouch a sycophantic throng,

Whose fears confess all rights to him belong.

For his delight alone the slaves provide.

An abject people strive their griefs to hide;

While, urged by selfish lusts, the rich and strong

Oppress the weak and poor with cruel wrong,

Till every natural birthright is denied.

The King of kings resigns celestial state

To bear our burdens, all our sickness cure;

To bless because we need, though not deserve.

Foreboding downfall to the haughty great,

His own example proves this precept sure:

Who would be chief among you, let him serve.

THE SNARE OF RICHES.

Good master: What shall make salvation sure?

Why call'st me good? There is none good but One.

Keep the commandments. So I've ever done.

One thing thou lackest to make all secure:

Sell all thou hast, divide among the poor,

The snare of great possessions thus to shun,

With me the race of self-denial run,

And treasure thou shalt have that will endure.

Sadly the young man left. How hardly they

Who trust in riches, find the narrow way!

But ye, who have left all to follow me,

In the regeneration, kings shall be.

Though persecution be your lot to-day,

Your recompense shall last eternally.

GOD'S DWELLING-PLACE.

Jehovah infinite, where dwellest thou?

Not highest heaven, nor hell's profoundest deep,

Nor widest bounds of earth thy presence keep,—

A true Shechinah where mankind may bow.

What outward altar bears thy sanction now,

Where heart-sick penitence may kneel and weep,

And soul-reviving faith with joy may leap,

Or fear may pay its mercenary vow?

Oh, pious pilgrim, seeking holy lands

For traffic in religion's market-place,

Sad relic thou of priestcraft's waning art.

God dwelleth not in temples made with hands:

Pure spirit hath no fellowship with space.

God dwelleth only in the human heart.

There's much beyond your present reach of thought.

The highest truths by time are slowly taught.

Obedience, clear discernment will confer,

And I will send the true interpreter,

The Paraclete replete with gospel sooth.

He shall develop insight into truth,—

Now dimly seen as in a darkened glass,—

That all your former knowledge shall surpass.

The world makes out no inkling of my aims;

Thinks esoteric truths mere empty names.

The world believes what outward eye commands,

What can be handled with material hands;

Such things as perish in their present use.

The ripening fruits their husks have helped produce.

We take the fruit but leave the husk behind.

The parables and fables of our youth,

If inwardly digested yield some truth

To nourish the maturer growth of mind.

But when he takes those leading-strings for guides,

The man his childhood's hobby-horse bestrides.

DAILY PROVIDENCE.

God hears the ravens when they cry for food;
Which neither sow nor reap nor store uplay.
Are ye not better than the feathered brood?

Why take ye thought for raiment? Lilies fair
Nor toil nor spin to win their bright array.
Are ye not worthier his watchful care?

Then waste no thought on mere external things,
With grovelling care to wear each weary day.
God knows your need and timely succor brings.

If think you must, think on life's broken vow.
Think on sweet charities; on others' claims.
But for the morrow take no thought. Live now.

To-morrows, when they come, will be to-days.
Seek first God's kingdom. Other lesser aims
The one thing needful largely underlays.

KEEPING THE SABBATH.

Woman, thou'rt loosed from thine infirmity.

Out-spake the sacristan indignantly,

Six days for labor: come then and be healed.

Thou hypocrite, dost let thy cattle thirst?

Wouldst let this woman suffer? Which ranks first?

Traditions of the elders are repealed.

Keep Sabbath strictly, save for mercy's needs.

Rest from your sins; but rest not from good deeds.

CHRIST'S FRIENDS.

Not they who say long prayers upon the street,

And give conspicuous alms, and fast in sight;

But whose left hand ignores the gracious right,

Whose faith is active; these my friends I greet.

LEADING MOTIVES.

Men fancy that pure reason is their guide,

When taste or passion or unreasoning pride

Determines all their course; and reason's task

Is but to hide the face with seemly mask.

OMNIPOTENCE.

But whence, if God is love and love is power,

Whence cometh hatred with its murderous train?

Whence avarice intent on selfish gain?

Whence pride that looketh down with haughty lower?

Whence crafty cunning keen to circumvent,

And meanness that with sneaking step doth cower,

And rapine ready peaceful plains to scour,

If God is love and love omnipotent?

. Omnipotence is not a brutal force. ˙

It doth not seize the sinner by the hair,[2]

And lift him bodily to purer air,

And all his imperfections thus endorse.

Omnipotence displays his mastery

By leading skilfully through hopes and fears,

Till, thus indulged, the manikin appears

The arbiter of his own destiny.

LIFE'S OVERFLOW.

The life divine, that floods the human soul,

Is infinite in finite boundary.

A sea between quite narrow banks may roll

If no obstruction check its passage free.

But let Niagara encounter rocks;

And furious foam attends the thundering shocks.

Selfhood, still unsubdued by discipline,

Would every privilege appropriate;

While other selfhoods set up claims as great,

Other Niagaras that rush en masse

To gain precedence, each at the same pass:

Earthquakes, whirlwinds, chaos; mingle their din.

In the far future, when we stand redeemed,

The conflicts of experimental life

Will seem like phantoms which our childhood dreamed, -

Unreal as the playground's mimic strife.

GOD'S LIKENESS.

To passing glance though goodness make no sign
On many a careless, many a careworn face,
The kindly eye of sympathy may trace
Distinctive traits of lineage divine.
A precious gem, concealed in darksome mine,
Betrays no token of its native grace,
Till searching light reveals its hiding-place,
And vests it with the privilege to shine.

Discords develop latent harmonics.
The frown of night involves the cheerful day.
A rugged husk the ripening fruit implies.
The all-creative Love, himself to please,
Shall mould his image from our common clay,
And make his likeness shine through human eyes.

CHRIST'S LAMENTATION OVER JERUSALEM.

Jerusalem, Jerusalem, how oft,

With kindlier care than brooding nature brings,

Would I have sheltered you beneath the wings

Of Mercy's dove, than mother's breast more soft.

But ye would not. My proffered love ye scoffed.

Daily your priests profane God's holy things.

Self-righteous scorn upon the lowly flings

High looks from where it proudly sits aloft.   .

Behold, your desolation draweth nigh.

Armies shall compass your devoted walls.

One stone upon another shall not stay.

But think ye that's the worst? I tell you nay.

The wrath of man is meant to typify

The desolation of a soul that falls.

WASHING THE DISCIPLES' FEET.

Then supper o'er, the Lord a towel took,
Poured water and began to wash their feet.
Lord, dost thou stoop our lowest wants to meet?
Cried Peter, with amazement in his look.
The act your reverence now can hardly brook
Hereafter shall with wisdom prove replete.
Again,—to check persistence indiscreet,—
The names of those I wash make up God's book.

Then Jesus said : Know ye what I have done?
Ye call me Lord and Master. That is true.
If I your Master never have abhorred
The meanest offices for every one,
Let my example teach you what to do.
The servant is not greater than his Lord.

THE AGONY.

The garden of Gethsemane by night
Concealed his agony from mortal sight.
Abba, my Father, all the power is thine.
Remove from me, I pray, this bitter cup.
But if with this last trial I must sup,
Drain to the dregs this cup of wrathful wine,
Then let thy mighty patience bear me up,
And let thy holy will be done, not mine.

THE BETRAYAL.

A mob, with swords and staves as 'gainst a thief,
Then came upon him. Judas was their chief.
He'd given them a sign they could not miss:
Hail, master; and betrayed him with a kiss.

Arch-traitor of the world, go to thy place.
Hell hath no further use for thee on earth.
The fiends, whose counsel gave thy treason birth,
Await thy coming, pleased with thy disgrace.

NON-RESISTANCE.

Put up thy sword or perish by the sword.
Think you I could not now my Father pray
Legions of angels succor to afford?
But then the Scriptures how could we obey,
And man be saved from suicide of soul?

The conqueror only maketh war to cease
When utter desolation bringeth peace.
God's conquests must preserve the conquered whole;
Change enemies to friends with their consent,
And leave them with submission well content.

MOCK TRIAL.

They led him to the high-priest to be tried.
Hypocrisy and priestcraft formed the court.
The proof false witnesses, self-falsified.
Verdict and sentence followed swift and short.

THE DENIAL.

Alas, the follower the Lord first chose,

The one he saved when boisterous waves arose,

Ordained the Spirit's mouth-piece to reveal

"Thou art the Christ;" Peter, the rock, all zeal;

Heaven's janitor; a witness to recount

The glorious transformation on the mount;

The first to draw the sword, true to the death;

This man denied the Lord with lying breath.

And Jesus turned and looked on Peter, mute.

But that grieved look, more eloquent than wrath,

The perjured bosom pierced with pang acute

Of deep remorse; to be assuaged in bath

Not of weak tears, but blood, soon to be shed

By that kind heart which suffers in our stead.

ASCENT OF CALVARY.

He is delivered to be crucified.
And now his manly shoulders meekly bow
Beneath another's load.   With patient stride
He slowly climbs, skull-mount, thy frowning brow.

Not unlike Samson, the strong Nazarite,
Clambering high Hebron's hill, with Gaza's gates
Ponderous upon his iron-sinewed back.
Yet most unlike: for in that cross unite
Enough of mortal sins and human hates
To sink the world; should his endurance lack.

THE CRUCIFIXION.

As Moses lifted up the serpent, so
The Son of man was lifted up, to show
How well he loved the world, and meant to draw
All men to him, by love's attractive law.

The sensual serpent of the human heart,
To heal, not hurt, may henceforth fill. its part.
Man's lower nature now may pure uprise,
Like Christ, his prototype, to native skies.

In his own -body on the cursed tree
Christ bare our sins, our captive souls to free.
Vain self must die with him, and pride be slain,
If we with him for evermore would reign.

Eloi, Eloi, lama sabachthani?

My God, my God, why hast thou forsaken me?

Jesus, thou Lamb of God, who tak'st away

The sins o' the world, by thine atonement true,

Teach us thy last triumphant prayer to say:

Father, forgive, they know not what they do.

Infinite love! divine humility!

We bow down to the dust; we worship thee.

Oh, what are all the pomp and power of kings,

Beside the majesty of self-control,

That, asking nothing, gives its very soul

To ransom men, the thoughtless, thankless things.

.

.

'Tis finished, the beloved Redeemer cried.

Then bowed the head of innocence, and died.

What's finished?   Literalism prompt replies:

The foreordained vicarious sacrifice.

Innocence executed in guilt's place!

No other way to save a ruined race!

Untutored savages reject the tale.

Nor with an upright child can it prevail

Until he be most diligently schooled,

His native sense of right and wrong o'erruled.

Christ died the just for the unjust, as though

He took our place, our death to undergo.

To save our lives the Lord his life resigned;

Yet not in lieu of vengeance due mankind.

Palpable contradiction, haste will say.

Impatience, pass along thy blundering way.

HUMAN ERROR.

Appearances a *tabula rasa* find
In the fresh field of undeveloped mind.
To such intelligence mistakes are sure.
But time and labor every fault will cure.

God's patience calmly bears with man's mistakes,
As age by age dull faculty awakes.
Mistakes are stepping-stones to human growth.
Without them man stands still in brutish sloth.
So have some stood a thousand weary years,
Hugging delusive hopes and foolish fears.

Awake, thou sleeper, rise and leave the dead,
As Christ hath risen. Follow in his tread,
And he shall give thine understanding, light
Wisely to walk, and not as fools by night,
Still stumbling o'er traditions men have taught,
But sharing in the freedom Christ hath bought.

I am the truth, the life, the only way;·

By following me ye cannot go astray.

I sanctify myself for others' sake,

That they through truth may holiness partake.

I go before you to prepare your place,

That where I am my friends may see my face.

The name of Jesus highest glory wins,

For he shall save his people from their sins.

Christ came into the world not to condemn

Weak men, but by all means to rescue them.

God was in Christ the world to reconcile

Unto himself, not from himself to exile.

At-one-ment reconciliation means

Of man to God, not God to his poor weans.

Christ died, not in our place, but for our sake,

To teach us how to die, and how to wake,—

To die to self, and wake to brotherhood,

To bury sin, and rise in all that's good,

To crucify the flesh with every lust,

And resurrect the soul in all that's just.

In the regeneration follow Christ,
Though every dearest wish be sacrificed.
Each step he took must be by us retrod.
Whom the Lord loves he greets with chastening rod.

Why hath it taken twice a thousand years
To unfold a truth you say so plain appears?
The *facts* were true two thousand years ago.
The *truth* of fact few minds then cared to know.

Wayfaring men in practice need not err:
The truthful heart's their safe interpreter.
But the deep things that angels look into,
Demand a cultured intellectual view.

And even now few delve in wisdom's mine.

To mere external things most men incline.

Science and mammon nigh monopolize

The keenest intellects with projects bold,—

Railroads and ships and banks and merchandise,

Law, medicine, inventions manifold.

What time have they for visionary cares?

Let priests and women traffic in such wares.

Yet these grandees well-weighed opinions claim,

And seem quite jealous for their pious fame.

Through slight confusion in the use of terms

Opinions grand mere prejudice affirms.

False pride and indolence perpetuate

Errors inherited with family plate.

Church councils have determined on the creed.

True faith is settled now beyond debate.

For peace and quiet thanks to happy fate.

Of controversy there's no further need.

From worry about doubtful doctrines freed,

The heart its own elysium may create,

With unconcern enjoy its present state,

And no intrusive questionings impede.

Nothing is settled save that God is true,

Though every man should prove a living lie.

For God there's nothing old and nothing new.

For man arrest of progress means to die.

To live is still to gain a wider view,

Till new horizons reach beyond the sky.

THE BURIAL.

They sadly laid him in the new-made tomb,

And went their way in silence and in gloom.

All hope seemed lost; the Lamb of God was slain;

And all his painful travail seemed in vain.

THE RESURRECTION.

On the third morn three women came alone.

An angel-hand had rolled away the stone.

On entering in they met a youth who said:

Seek not the living here among the dead.

He's risen. See the place where he was laid.

Trembling they fled, for they were sore afraid.

To the disciples, when they came all pale,

Their wondrous words seemed like an idle tale,

Which they believed not, till the Lord appeared,

And with salaam of peace their spirits cheered.

EASTER.

Why bursts all nature forth in sudden bloom,
Tree, hedge, and river-bank with blossoms bright,
Perfuming all the air, that yester-night
Still shrieked in tones recalling Winter's gloom?
'Tis Easter morn. The dark and dismal tomb,
Emblem of death, who touches but to blight,
No longer holds the Lord of life and light.
Therefore doth Spring her gala dress resume.

Grouped into garlands gay of human flowers,
The happy children, with united voice,
Pour forth a chorus of triumphant song.
What theme, I pray, inspires their tuneful powers?
The Lord is risen: let the earth rejoice,
And joyful echoes let the heavens prolong.

THE ASCENSION.

He led them forth as far as Bethany.
Raising his hands, he blessed them. While he blessed,
The heavens received him. 'To eternal rest?
Nay, his vast work, the human race to free,

Was but begun. The boon of liberty,
Which all the rabid powers of hell contest,
And human tyranny has oft repressed,
Will claim his safeguard to eternity.

PREACHING THE GOSPEL.

To aid the arduous task that feeble band
Forth fared like lambs among a wolfish horde.
Hunted, imprisoned, scourged, put to the sword,
How can they hope the demons to withstand?

But though they have no courage of their own,
The Lord will send them succor from on high:
His unseen hand will be forever nigh;
He will not leave them comfortless—alone.

FINAL TRIUMPH.

Love's power is gentle, but exceeding strong.
The violence of man may work delay.
His stubborn will may seem God's hand to stay;
But patient Mercy waits and suffers long.

A thousand years with God are but a day.
A single day is like a thousand years.
Unswayed by human hopes or human fears,
His love at length will have its own lief way.

L'ENVOI.

Dear Master, might a novice see thy face,
As the disciples saw thee day by day,
While walking with thee, talking by the way
Of all the wonders of redeeming grace:
Thy looks of kind compassion might he trace,
While healing sickness, helping souls astray,
Blessing the children, teaching men to pray;
He would exclaim: God's house is in this place.

Thy wish is granted. Cast thine eyes around.
Unconscious smiles of innocence are mine.
Since God alone is good, where good is found
Thou findest me; where two their prayers combine,
There am I in the midst. Let love abound;
Be duty done; and life becomes divine.

NOTES.

1. Page 84.

"The man who can keep his science and his religion in two boxes, either of which may be opened separately, is to be congratulated." Review of Le Conte's " Evolution and Religious Thought."—*The Nation. No. 1202.*

2. Page 95.

"God doth not drag the struggling creature, by the hair of the head, up to his own impracticable heights."—*Henry James, Sr.*

www.ingramcontent.com/pod-product-compliance
Lightning Source LLC
Chambersburg PA
CBHW032102010726
47493CB00008B/2494